Seasons of an Irish Hermitage

Seasons of an Irish Hermitage

Proceeds from this book go to feed the hungry and
clothe the naked. We thank you for your purchase.

To see some of our other products, go to
www.xanga.com/sistersofgraceofchrist

ISBN: 978-0-9809317-1-6

Seasons of an Irish Hermitage

by a Nun of Grace

Introduction...

*Nestling into the green-shawled breast
on an Irish mountain a small
hermitage hides...*

*Reached only by a bridge, it is girded
on the other three sides by water... two
fast-flowing streams and the wide,
restless sea...*

*Trees shelter it lovingly... old native
ash and alder, rowan and willow;
hawthorn and fuchsia hedge it...*

*Here dwells a Nun, a Monastic
Solitary, living apart from her Order in
a work of cloistered Prayer.*

*Sister wears the full, traditional
Monastic Habit of her Order. Full-
length, black habit, deep blue scapular,*

1

white guimp and large white wimple, and her veil is long, deep blue lined with white.

In these modest garments, she is known and visibly a Nun.

The skills of her hands in her seclusion support the care of the homeless, especially children, in many lands where her Sisters in Christ Jesus live out their calling among the most needy of mankind...

Her outgoings are few, for essentials only, her visitors fewer. Her love for others expressed in her separation...

Hers are the seasons, the flowers and food she tends in her gardens... the wild flowers... Hers the first birdsong of the day, the last sweet vespers they linger in…

Hers too are the creatures who enrich her life… Those no one wants, like the little ones her Sisters care for… the lost, the sick, the crippled…

These reflections and stories and poems are single threads in a tapestry woven and stitched over many years.

Single blossoms in a bouquet… gleanings and gatherings along the quiet lanes of the years.

The seasons of the Irish year, of the Church, of nature, closely interwoven as they are.

Above and in all they reflect the heart-life of a Monastic Nun, to whom everything becomes prayer.

3

I hold in my hands a star
Its vibrant light lifting it from palms
Which curve to cherish it.

I keep in my heart a joy,
A pause of eternity –
Caught from the silent hours.

My hands and my heart are vessels
Weak and frail as the tiniest shell
Caught in the swell of endless tides..
Launched against shores of jagged
rocks
Helpless in the rhythm of the earth

My hands must hold other things,
Move from their curve of prayer
To other things.

Yet He is there
In my hands and heart,
The miracle..

And He will not move though I move

Contents

Beginnings...

Nightfall came early on Epiphany.

A gloomy, grey-drab January day, skies heavy and lowering.

As the last light faded in the sky over the sea, Sister resolutely "took Christmas down."

The figures from the Crib were carefully, lovingly, enfolded in tissue paper, and laid within the stable at the bottom of its cardboard box.

The holly, dry now and shriveled, she burnt on the fire.

It crackled and spat as it flamed blue. A last brightness.

All the red silk poinsettias... all the candles...

Shrouded in their tissue and packed away neatly.

The Advent Wreath greenery joining the holly on the blazing turf fire.

All was stripped bare, cleaned and cleared.

It always looked so bare.

And Sister sighed.

Especially at this dark, drab season. When winter still had many weeks to run, and rain seemed constant.

Even the cats hated to go out and were

spending most of their time asleep by the fire or on her bed.

Great black and white furballs…

Even though the shortest day was past, and the birdsong was more alive – still it was the very depths of winter.

The ground was sodden; too waterlogged to dig, and keen icy winds crept in between clothing, making outings to the shore less attractive. Sister sighed, then shook herself. This would not do at all, at all!

She fetched the old toasting fork, cut bread thick and chunky, and made toast on the glowing fire… spread it generously with butter and blackberry jam, redolent of autumn days, and feasted.

Feeling decidedly more cheerful, she resolutely picked up the boxes and opened the large, deep cupboard under the stairs, where the Christmas cartons were stored the year round.

As she was putting them in, a stack of smaller boxes caught her eye.

Intrigued, she pulled them out.

All were full of papers she had stored.

She had not looked at them for a long while.

Had even forgotten they were there.

So she took them back to the fire, settled snug in her armchair, and started to read.

Files of poems, stories, reflections,
recipes, patterns.

Things written, others garnered from
other books, over many years.

Some hand written on yellowed paper,
others printed out from her faithful old
laptop.

Quotations that had caught her eye.

Prayer cards from dear ones long gone
home now.

Always she had intended to sort and
collate them.

But somehow there had just never been
time or chance to do it, and so the
collection had grown.

Well, now there was maybe time to do this...

She straightened up, resolution strong.

Yes; a good time while the year lay low.

An absorbing task when there was time and space for it.

And the cats wandered down the stairs, squirrel-furred tails held high in question marks, as if sensing the sudden energy.

"Ah, I suppose you want food?" as they arched against her..."Or just attention? Or both?"

It was several minutes before there was peace again.

A tin of cat food to be opened and dispensed, while they purred and leaned against her so hard it was a difficult task.

Caro leaping onto the table…butting her with his head…making her laugh with his ardour.

Before the cats, replete with food and affection, were once more in a furry heap before the fire, sprawled in total trust and surrender. Eyes closed, tails wrapped over their noses.

Before Sister, lamps lit in the firelight, and soft rain musical against the window, could return to her new task.

"Let me see," she mused. "I will set the recipes and patterns aside…and the quotations and prayer cards too."

Of course, she was waylaid many times, caught up in something she had forgotten she had written...

"This is as bad as trying to light the fire with old newspapers," she mused aloud.

Amanda lifted her head at her voice, looked up, stretched out a white-socked paw, then yawned, and yielded to sleep once more.

The thick files of papers went back many years.

It seemed hard at first to classify them. Then she saw that many were seasonal, so that seemed the way to go.

So a pile for spring, one for summer... and so on...

"A potpourri," she murmured. "A collage for each season."

And so it was...

Echoing the seasons of the earth, and the seasons and great festivals of the Church also.

Unfolding, enfolding. Dark, light. Shadow and sunlight.

Each in its right place and time.

Part One...

...the Promise

The Promise...

The New Year is a pure, white unwritten page.

Open, vulnerable... above all a promise.

Of infilling and growing. Of life and joy.

Of seeding and nurturing.

Of fullness and flowering, of fruiting and harvest.

The trees are bare, yet if you run gentle, sensitive fingers along the desolate, stark twigs, the leaves are there, small buds under the bark.

Small shoots of snowdrops and crocus peep out from the dark, lonely soil.

Always the promise.

Yet still a time for firelight and early darkfall.

Dark hours, and short days…

Yet slowly light gaining over darkness.

A time that will end with new lambs, daffodils, and Lenten days.

A time of anticipation, of dry seeds and sap rising.

Of hopes and plans, of dreams and unspoken yearnings.

Of heart-prayers too tender to speak.

A time too when the fruits of the year that has gone still feed and warm us...

When we yearn and long for light as we keep warm by fireside.

The old ways of wood and peat, earth-heart.

Beech branches blazing in the wide old
hearth;

Seasoned in long years, clean-
fragranced.
Grateful warmth released with sap-
song humming...
Glowing in ashes.

Light fading slowly now in a bright,
light sky.
Trees barely moving; peace upon all.

And the birds... Robin and wren, stalwart songsters of the long winter, throng the air with renewing melodies.

Sister smiled as she heard the wren that morning.

The sweetest song, and the tiny dapper bird from whose throat such beauty emerged so effortlessly.

And read the journal story from times past.

Smiling at the memories it evoked, of a young cat rescued, and cherished as long as he lived.

The Cat and the Wren

Hunter Cat, whose full story has yet to be told, was young, and learning all the time, often the painful experiential learning that young things specialize in.

Like learning that fire hurts, by touching a candle flame.

However many times a youngling is told that, it really only sinks in when they have been hurt.

And so it was with Hunter Cat.

He was never still for long, and always in trouble of some kind.

Always learning the hard way.

His chief love in life, after food, and Sister, was to chase and, sadly, too often catch, anything that crawled or flew.

The pigmy shrew population had shrunk since his coming.

The poor wee things have to eat every two hours to survive.

So they are around all day.

Sister had lost count of the number that had raced in through the door like a scrap of wind blown fluff, to take refuge under the settee before Hunter Cat skidded in in hot pursuit.

And of the times she had rescued one, wet from the jaws of death, and set it down in the vegetable patch, safe behind netting to recover.

Wriggling in the safe palm of her hand.

Hunter Cat would creep up through the lower branches of bushes to seize any unwary bird.

Until one day, Sister heard a loud crashing noise and ran to the door to find him on the ground, looking dazed.

He had learned the hard way that he was now too big and heavy for the bushes to sustain his weight. Spatial awareness was not his forte.

Always after the birds of course, and trying to get to the clever platform

Sister had contrived so the tiny feathered ones she loved could still feed without risking their lives.

It was suspended on thin cords, and would unceremoniously dump anything larger than a thrush that landed on it.

While she knew it was just nature, there was no way Sister was going to stand by and watch this murder if she could help avoid it.

But she forgave much the night the young cat fought and caught the large rat she had heard scurrying in the roof space.

It had grown bold and made a hole through the thick stone wall, and then eaten through the plaster to steal the cats' food.

Poison was not possible, and nor were traps large enough for a rat, for Hunter Cat would no doubt get a paw or a nose hurt.

One dark night Sister was startled awake by a screaming and a thudding from below.

Heart in her mouth, and a prayer on her lips, she crept down the stairs and with great courage, as the silence thickened, she slowly opened the door.

There was blood, it seemed, everywhere.

And by the body of a large, dead rat, Hunter Cat stood, shaking in his furry boots.

Nothing he had preyed on had ever fought back, of course. And once battle was engaged, there was no turning back without injury.

The phrase a fight to the death held new meaning.

Sister removed the corpse on the shovel, shuddering as she did so, and threw it far into the bushes.

Wiped the stains away with bleach.

All at two o'clock in the morning...

Then she made a hot drink, opened a tin of tuna, and gathered up the shivering cat to retreat to bed.

The bond between them was strong, and he was soon comforted and purring, as she congratulated and thanked him...

And fed him the food he loved most of all.

Then he snuggled in with Sister for the rest of the night.

When Hunter Cat was still small, he would obey her and stop running when she called. After all, he had been with her since he was around three weeks old, so she was his mother and his boss...

But that was changing rapidly now, as he realized that she would take his prey off him. And it was no use him clamping his jaws tight, as she had the knack of forcing them open.

And all the while yelling at him.

And oh, could Sister yell!

And right in his sensitive ears — as she well knew.

One sweet, mild February day, she was sitting at the door when he fled past, and she saw that his mouth was full of feathered life.

Still moving.

So she gave chase, and in the confusion, Hunter Cat fled into the house.

Big mistake!

He was cornered, and loosened his grip just enough for the bird to fly free.

Whereupon Hunter Cat was firmly and loudly evicted and the door shut on him.

And no amount of pressing his face against the window and wailing availed.

The tiny wren, for such it was, the sweetest songster in the garden, fled up the wide chimney. The fire was thankfully not yet lit, so Sister assumed it had flown up and out.

And was thus startled later when out it flew again.

It had simply found a safe dark place to rest and recover in.

So she opened the door, making sure Hunter Cat was not near, and gently ushered it out into the free air.

And that, so she thought, was that.

Not so.

Hunter Cat was about to meet his match, in the form of the tiny wren he had caught.

A few days later, Sister's peace at prayer was totally disrupted by the loudest, longest bird alarm call she had ever heard.

When she went downstairs, and realized what was happening, she settled in the sheltered corner by the door to watch.

Stifling laughter with increasing difficulty.

It was almost beyond belief.

Hunter Cat was lying all but hidden in last year's dead grass in the wild part of the garden.

His coat was mottled and barred, ideal camouflage. Under normal circumstances, that is.

All but hidden, as in the tree directly above him, the wren sat, scolding at the top of her voice, indignantly berating the cat.

He moved elsewhere – and the wren followed him, safe in the tree tops and still scolding.

She became like a Geiger counter, increasingly loud as he approached.

Wherever Hunter Cat tried to hide, to lie

in wait for some unsuspecting bird, there she was.

And of course no bird would come near…. They all knew an alarm call when they heard it, and respected and obeyed it totally.

After nearly an hour, Hunter Cat had no choice but to give up. He stalked indoors, with a look of defeat and disgust on his expressive face.

And always after that, whenever he tried to lie in ambush, there the wren would be.

A tiny, indignant scrap of life with a family to raise.

He had little chance of catching anything.

He took then to sleeping most of the day, to emerge at night, when the wren was snug asleep in her nest.

And a cat could hunt decently without interruption.

Maybe that is why cats are nocturnal.

Sister always wondered how he came by the young hare with no head she found near the old car...

But his story is one for another time.

Sister sat a while after reading this. Memories filling her mind and heart.

"Odd," she mused, "How vivid memory is. I can almost hear the wren scolding."

Then she sat up.

"I CAN hear the wren scolding!"

As she stood quickly up, in, through the window, flew Amanda, round green eyes huge and flashing in her black face, and her mouth full of feathered life.

While outside it seemed every bird in the area was scolding and raising the alarm.

Sister could hardly catch the cat for laughing.

And this tiny one lived to fly another day.

And to joy the early hours with her sweet song.

Sister worked on, reading and sorting until Grand Silence heralded Compline.

Pondering the beauty of these early months of the year in the dark stillness.

And always knowing that as soon as there was a glimmer of light, the throbbing songs of so many birds would slowly build once more to a glorious crescendo.

That as these last weeks of winter spent themselves, more and more would join the melody; that she would listen for each new note and tone with held breath.

Birdsong loud now.
Many-throated...

Staunch winter stalwarts still,
Robin, wren,

Their airs daily joying the dark months.

Simple notes of blue-tits.

The dove-cooing of pigeons, soothing,
full.

Stark, startling cry of pheasant,
Raucous in still air.

Listening for the cuckoo now,

Watching the skies for the first
swallow,

Heralds fulfilling faithful promise.

Other notes rising now.

Thrush, blackbird...
Warblers...

Living hearts bursting with life
and joy.

Singing praise to the Living Lord.

His love is soft lace, enfolding the
heart,
Delicate, intricate - simple as light.

His love is the daffodils, dancing
delight.

His love is the young lambs, butting for
food,
Fleece-curly, tails wagging, full of His
life!

His love is the dust-seeds, buried in
earth,
With promise of burgeoning carrots and
flowers

His love is the evening, darkening
blessed,
Birds hushing, wind easing, calmly to
night.

His love is a warm bed at long day's
hard end;
Welcoming, beckoning, "Come, rest,
dear child.
Lay down your tired head; sleep safe
in My Heart.
Fear nothing; protected by angels of
Mine."

And Lent lay ahead, its pleached ways
echoing the dark winter that was
passing.

Lent Reflection

Lent… a time for turning...and for loving.

Life is full of turnings. Of changes. Many we do not choose; these, the growing and the ageing, are in God's plans, as the changing of the seasons and skies.

All these are in God's loving hands alone.

But sometimes we need to choose; to consent, to embrace. Some turnings are those yearnings towards God that stir deeply within our souls and bring soft tears to our eyes, we know not why.

Lent is such a time. See it not as deprivation.

It is a self-emptying so that God can fill us with Himself, and with that love He holds for us and for all His creation.

See it not as a giving up, but as a gaining.

A turning towards Him.

Which means a turning away from all that is not Him or of Him.

So we turn away from the "world" and its values and pursuits and ambitions.

We close off from its vanities and trivialities so we can focus on Him and all He bids us do.

We leave self behind - in order to find selfhood in Him.

And a time for loving...When you love, oh yes; when you have hurt who you love, or Who you love, for all pain caused to others is pain to Him Who loves all, then there is inner hurt and weeping.

So we mourn over our sin, over our lack of loving for God and for all His people, and thus we seek forgiveness...

And then we amend our lives; for unless our contrition and our penitence change our ways, then they are sterile and selfish.

He is our Creator; we are made in His image so strive we to be true to His purity in loving.

He is our Baby; so strive we to nurture and protect Him in all the vulnerable.

He is our Lord, so strive we to obey His Word.

He is our Brother, so strive we as He calls us to be kin to all, as He is.

All in the Light of Love.

And if we hold back, then that is sin.

And in these blessed and holy days of Lent, we can bring that failing to Him on the knees of the humility of our helplessness and our need of His grace.

So lacerate your heart for your lack of love - then let the balm of His grace and mercy soothe and heal - and let His love for all His creation saturate and permeate your whole being and lives and actions, and spread and widen to cover and fill the whole world and all in it.

Then we shall be the salt, the yeast, the light, the love that Jesus bids us be - and only with His help and starting with our willingness to turn and to be turned.

We can align with that love; that is a choice we can make with our wills; then let Him act in and through us.

So Lent as a journey; as a taking into ourselves more of Him.

Not just for the Forty Days, but for life.

New ways, new habits.

Away from the world's values...
towards the teachings of Jesus...

Strong, positive.

Isaiah speaks of "true fasting"...

"Is this the kind of fast I have chosen,
only a day for a man to humble
himself?
Is it only for bowing one's head like a
reed
and for lying on sackcloth and ashes?
Is that what you call a fast,
a day acceptable to the LORD ?

Is not this the kind of fasting I have
chosen:
to loose the chains of injustice
and untie the cords of the yoke,
to set the oppressed free
and break every yoke?

Is it not to share your food with the
hungry and to provide the poor
wanderer with shelter-
when you see the naked, to clothe him,
and not to turn away from your own
flesh and blood?

Then your light will break forth like the
dawn,
and your healing will quickly appear;
then your righteousness will go before
you,
and the glory of the LORD will be your
rear guard.

Then you will call, and the LORD will
answer;
you will cry for help, and he will say:
Here am I.
If you do away with the yoke of
oppression,

with the pointing finger and malicious
talk,

And if you spend yourselves in behalf
of the hungry
and satisfy the needs of the oppressed,
then your light will rise in the darkness,
and your night will become like the
noonday.

The LORD will guide you always;
he will satisfy your needs in a sun-
scorched land
and will strengthen your frame.
You will be like a well-watered garden,
like a spring whose waters never fail.

Your people will rebuild the ancient
ruins
and will raise up the age-old
foundations;

you will be called Repairer of Broken
Walls,
Restorer of Streets with Dwellings."

A purposeful giving.... not a self-
centred one.

And thus the emphasis on "sin" that so
many find hard.

See "sin" is simply a failing in loving;
in loving God, in loving each other.
Thus that great penitential Psalm 51
says, "Against Thee only have I
sinned."

There is in the west of Ireland a Holy
Mountain. Croagh Patrick.

And it is a symbol of Lent; for Lent is
a symbol of life in Christ.

Leading to Easter, to Light, to
Resurrection and eternity.

A passage, not a destination.

It is a mile of steep rocky path, littered
with stones, rock-strewn... Marked by
the Stations of the Cross.

Many walk it barefoot. Some even on
their knees.

And so in life, we meet many fellow-
pilgrims on the way..

And Jesus tells us to love them as we
love ourselves.

How often we shy away from the
fullness of that...

Hence Isaiah...

Lean towards them. Lend a helping hand...

Give all you can - not of your abundance but of your substance.

And always, upwards.

And always towards the Cross at the top.

Mark the steps in prayer; mark the days with an extra giving; of time; of resources; for all means loving Him more and more each day.

A giving to Christ, Who gave His life, when we give what we value most.

And we show this with our bodies and our substance, because Christ became

man and lived as we do - a giving life -
a giving death.

So Lent. A giving; a marking... A
turning...

And let this be not just for Lent; but for
always.

Saint Francis knew the truth of this; he
who embraced Lady Poverty to own
nothing.
And embraced a leper "... that we seek
not so much to be consoled as to
console... not so much to be loved as to
love... For it is in giving that we receive."

That seemingly-contradictory truth that
is the very heart of Christ.

And that thus separates us from "the
world" and its materialistic values.

Let us each this Lent lean towards our fellow-pilgrims, when they stumble on stones let us reach out a hand to steady them.

When they are hungry, feed them...

For as Jesus teaches, then we feed Him (Matthew 25)

So, in practice?

For we are always so ready to nod and agree, but then know not the how of it.

That can be hard.

And following Jesus is a very practical way to walk.

If you give up eating something, set aside a set sum for each day.

Aim at children? At famine relief?

Let any so-slight hunger we might feel feed those whose stomachs ache with the need for food that is not there.

If you give up doing; let it work for others...Clear out cupboards and let a charity shop benefit... Catch up on letters to old friends who may need a kind word... give time and strength to a voluntary scheme, or practical kindness to a lonely or elderly neighbour...

And above all, pray; not intercession but simply spending time in rapt silence with Him Who loves us so much. Love Him, and be still with Him.

And why stop when Lent ends?

Let your turning be eternal...Let it build strength in your soul...

Let it bring you ever closer and closer to God.

For once you have glimpsed and tasted that closeness, you will never turn away again.

So although the track may be rocky and rough, is not the goal so precious that that matters not?

So let Lent be a joy, a deeply meaningful growing time.

And when Easter dawns you will be nearer Him and stronger in spirit and in truth...

Then turn not away again... Turn not your back on Him.. Return not to the world's ways...keep your eyes on Him, gaze always at the Cross.

The season turned, the evenings stretching out now even as Lent deepened and progressed.

Sister always thought how strange it was, that Lent came when the year was burgeoning breathlessly.

When it seemed each day brought new flowers and leaves, when her walk to the shore almost each day led between banks where wood sorrel was a blizzard, then wild violets, and always in these days, pale, pure-faced primroses.

When the fields were filling with tiny new lambs.

And the great festival here that was Saint Patrick's Day.

When the streets were filled with
Marches and processions.

And the traditional music, often the
three-piece band of fiddle flute and
accordion raised the rafters at Masses
where the Gaelic was heard.

New clothes, decked with sprays of
shamrock, and feasting replacing
fasting.

All held in the growing towards the
great light of Easter.

As the Advent Candles increased the
light also.

Promise of light and hope and life in
all around and in all within.

Part Two…

…the Fulfilment

Easter Even...

The Lighting of the Paschal Candle.

The sharp dawn in the still breath
The Christ-light in the pure faith
Candle leading candle
Light giving light
All to all.

Dark figures clothed in light
Depth of dark giving light
Strength of spark-light shedding dark
All from all.

Moving light star-studded
Glowing warmth fanning life
Glow-light spreading
All in all.

Sister remembered the poignant time
when that poem was written.

Her eyes misted as she read it.

The time of her own calling to be a Nun.

A time so tender and so beautiful.

That night she had known fully and
irrevocably where she belonged.

She found other poems written at the
same time, each from her heart-bliss.

And reading them now filled her anew
with joy and deep gratitude.

Undiminished as she gazed back down
the decades of her life as a Nun.

Indeed increased as the fulfilment grew.

For the Light Jesus had lit in her heart that Easter Eve had grown and spread through her whole being and her whole life, as the candles in that Chapel.

The years had only added to its lustre, not dimmed or muted it.

His peace that night had promised and fulfilled that.

Hills calm create in the early gold,
Birds flying, twig-laden.
Flowers uncurling secret joy-
Calm and peace.

Pure holy voice in Chapel calm
White on gold, bright gold
Blooms caught in stillness
White and gold

Let me remember this hour forever
This hour of calm and green peace.

Birds questing for worms,
Singing in spring ardour...

Clouds of creative rain hovering...

Trees swaying...

Wind blowing fierce and free
Over gentle hills

Many Easters had passed since then, spent in many places and with many different folk.

In community, in solitude.

And often folk questioned her life set apart thus.

The reality and rightness and validity of it.

Her heart answered gently, for few understood.

Or ever would. And that was fine and right.

This life was a mystery, a given and a giving.

The Monasticism she and her Sisters lived was one untainted by passing ages. As true and as pure as in the early centuries after the coming of Jesus.

As relevant and real now as then.

So her heart always was gentle.

And her words quiet and telling in their sincerity, as she spoke of the life she lived as a Solitary Nun.

Of the life all Monastics live.

Hidden and apart.

Silence and Solitude

Music… the sough-sighing of the wind
in chimney-breast,
Buffeting strong, stone walls.

Purring of soft-furred cats.
Crooning of hens, bleating of sheep.

Night speaking stillness of
magnanimous stars,
Wheeling and whirling in time-tangling
dance.

Company…bird and beast,
Flowers and grass.

Walking with Jesus by day and by
night.

And in that night,

The hidden angels,
Rays of love beneficent.

Soft whisperings of wide feathered
wings,

Silent benedictions.

Always on Easter Night, for her a Vigil, wherever she was that night.

Whether alone or with other Sisters.

The first poem centred on the formal Easter Vigil when the Paschal Candle was lit from new fire in the Convent Chapel.

The first candles lit from that light were taken to the rows of Nuns and their small candles lit then.

And then to those who were spending Easter with them.

Passing the Light on, not hiding or hoarding it.

So that the Light was passed on and grew stronger and stronger as more flames burned bright.

Light defeating darkness, from the moment that first spark flared.

The theme from Genesis onwards…
"Let there be Light… and there was light."

One strange thing about light is that it takes only a tiny gleam, a single, small candle for it not to be dark any more.

Darkness is more fragile than light...

Every Easter now, Sister would keep Vigil; preferring the solitude and silence up on the mountain to one of the Dawn Masses that were so many now.

Setting a chair facing east, enfolded warm in her cloak.

Invisible, veiled and still.

In that intense darkness just before dawn.

Waiting, watching, cool air on her face as the pre-dawn wind rose.

Hands clasped in prayer.

Resting after Holy Week, and the heaviness of Good Friday.

Good Friday...darkness, suffering, abandonment, resonating through every heart...

The pain is raw, naked, and we can hardly bear to look at it...

Every suffering, every individual agony of body, mind, soul, is caught to that cry as with a strong, slender thread...

A huge, yet intimate web, intricate, yet so clear.

After the drear darkness and emptiness of Holy Saturday.

Watching for the Light.

Then the first, tiny, pale lightening.

The birds see and know it before human eye, and always Sister smiled at the first sleepy cheepings.

Warm, snug feathered ones, roused by the light.

And that small tenderness spread as the light grew and the crescendo of birdsong gathered living joy.

Outshining candle flame.

CHRISTOS ANESTI

ALLELUIA! ALLELUIA! ALLELUIA!

"He is not here; he is risen!"

And the year now filling and unfolding in the green and gold glory that was Ireland.

Sister fingered photos of hedgerows thick with blossom.

Bridal sprays of hawthorn.

Gorse so bright it hurt the eyes. Hiding the cruel thorns it bore.

Verges clouded with cow parsley and gilded with buttercups.

Remembering forest paths leading through fragrant, sky-fallen bluebells.

And a sheaf of poems…

May…

Sweet month of warmth and promise.

Burgeoning tenderness, fresh,
renewed…

Month of sweet blossoming,
Fair promise of fruiting.

Sacredness; silence.

Blessedness of birdsong.
Soft and peaceful in summer's fullness.
Content to be where Jesus has willed
them…

To be…

To laud Him with their given-voices.

Above, cloud-cover the feathering of
His wings,
Protecting, sheltering.
Soft, soft grey.

Alders, last to green, stirring but
slightly.

And He has veiled the mountains.

All is soft and muted; holy and sacred.
Praise His Name.....

High summer...

Stillness...

The rain has ceased its heavy orison.
Moisture clears slowly from the quiet
air.

Silence.

The sky holds its breath, as brightness
grows.
Waiting, watching; will the sun break
through?

Will clouds part? Azure reveal its
glory?

Will sky-weeping pause?

Will light and warmth once more
Ray and beam their benison on
upturned faces?

On hungry souls, prayer-food?

Tall alders barely move.
Just a tiny, fragile leaf-dance.

Stillness, silence.

The far mountains across the green
valley,
Hidden in rain for days
Mist slowly into view.

Even birds are hushed.
Waiting, watching,
For light after darkness,

Sun after rain,
Light after dark.

Sweet peas
And candlelight.

Rain thudding heavy from dark skies.
Down the chimney spattering.

View all vanished in the sheeting water.
Wind in tall trees

Sweet peas by candlelight...

Early day dawning...

Last light dapple-dancing, leaf-filtered.

Marigolds glowing still with sun's gold.
Birds hushed; cats safe in.
Food set ready for wild one's fare.
All hushed.

And, far away,
The world its evening seeks.
TV, unreal "reality,"
Bars full to brimming.
Unreality of alcohol.

Last light dancing amid green leaves,
Soft spirit breath there.
Reality.

Breathing Jesus alone up here.

Who the needy one?
Who the lonely one?
Who the poor?

Last light dancing.
Starlight glancing.

Somehow, the summer spoke in poems.
It was impossible to find words to
describe the utter life and beauty.

Nothing was filtered through human
eyes or voices, and the experience
became intense,

It was the time for the garden, for the
reliable miracle of seed and shoot.

Of seeing how to grow best, always
obeying and observing the rhythm of
season and time.

Because that was how it was made.

A gift that awed and humbled her to the
very heart.

And always in her heart, the knowledge and awareness of the needy world her Sisters tended, of the desperate poverty man had created by his perversion of the work of God.

Of the utter beauty and purity of the Master's hand..

Of the abundance of His grace and provision, if all shared and gave. Food enough for all, and to spare, pressed won and brimming over.

You left us to play in the garden You
gave us
Oh, such a fair fertile place….
You planted our feet in the good earth,
Our eyes fixed on You.

Fruit and flowers, birdsong too.
Inquisitive fur and feathers.
Whose bright eyes look to as, as we do
to You.
So that we echo You.

You gave us Rules..
Told how to do all.
How to nurture
How to cherish,
How to grow, to love.

How too to ignore the evil, slimey,
creeping things

What to eat, what not to eat.

Feet firm on earth, heart in the heavens.

When darkness that is not of You,
Nor of natural right, broke in
You taught us how to choose.

Gave us the brightness and newness of
children to nurture –
Copies of us, copies of You.
Keep their feet firm on earth,
Their hearts turn to Jesus.

Cherish, nurture, love
With the echoing of God's love.

Turn the suffering to giving,
Feet on earth, spirit seeking heaven.

You gave us, in love, a garden to play
in.

Help us to play!
To cherish, to nurture
To love with that echo of Your love for
us.
To choose freely to play in Your
garden.

Sister paused then, set the work aside.

Outdoors, walking the paths, gazing out to sea, drinking in the freshness and abundance of all around her, praying always.

It was all so fair and lovely, yet so fragile.

The leaves, full and rich now, the rows of neat vegetables, thriving.

Everywhere flowers.

Then back she wandered as the long evening deepened.

Refreshed and renewed, to eat and tidy, set the house to rights, feed her sheep and cats.

Before settling one last time to read and reflect.

And she smiled and laughed then as she fingered a small story from island days.

It was as vivid now as then. She could smell the fresh-pulled carrots, see the huge, bright, fragrant roots...

Of carrots and cabbages…

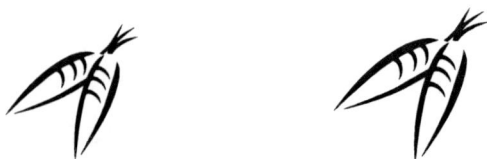

Summer days, and eating from the garden was now a daily joy, never taken for granted.

Rarely was any vegetable bought now. With planning, and thought, this was a natural rhythm.

The choice so far north and without a greenhouse was limited.

Cabbage, carrots, turnips, broad beans, peas… parsnips did well, and some years cauliflowers.

And the growing season was incredibly short.

Nothing could safely be planted out until May, and even then there was almost always a ferocious wind storm at the end of May or early June that could scorch and burn anything above ground.

So Sister concentrated now on good amounts of the staples, and as the years passed, grew to enjoy food in its true season.

And learned to freeze and dry enough to help during the long winter, when only cabbages and turnips were left.

The first new spring greens were a welcome and a celebration.

Living off the land had a harmony and an attraction.

So she started cabbages and other plants off in a light outbuilding, ready to set out when the danger of frost and gales was past.

And sold the surplus seedlings.

And always she was clearing more and more ground to grow more.

This year, she had flayed and dug a new patch, taking the grass off carefully.

It was painstaking work, but good to be out in the air in the early year, working in an ancient rhythm.

And a deep pleasure and satisfaction to dig deep and refine the earth, taking every stone and root out, to make a good bed for carrots.

Three times she dug the new patch. Three times she sifted the lumps through her fingers.

She brought sand up from the shore to mingle in and lighten the soil still further.

For good, straight carrots needed loose, clean soil. Else the growing roots forked and became stunted.

And this year her carrots more than repaid the work.

They germinated swift and true, and from then on, there was, as they say, no stopping them.

Some she pulled for salads and baby roots.

But most she left, after careful thinning, to fulfill their growth.

One day in late summer, she pulled one, just out of interest. Just to see what they were like now.

It was so big she just could not believe it, so she pulled another... the same... and then another, until half a row lay in her basket.

She was amazed at the size and weight of the sturdy, straight roots. Some weighed over half a pound.

They were lying in the kitchen awaiting cooking when a neighbour called round.

Iris was a frequent caller, and Sister delighted in serving her tea in her best china, out on the lawn, when the weather allowed, with the home baking that was a strong island tradition Sister wholeheartedly embraced.

The cats would come to be stroked, and the peacocks would stroll past, tails outspread and quivering.

There were flowers everywhere.

Sister knew Iris loved flowers, and that her house was too exposed to grow much.

So she would pick her a posy to take home.

A small piece of gracious living on an island where the weather made life harsh.

They talked of many things.

And when the conversation turned to the garden, Sister just could not resist telling how good her carrots were this year.

When she brought the bowl out..

The islanders were taciturn to a fault. Rarely would they give praise, to your face at any rate. And rarely did they thank for a gift.

So it spoke worlds when Iris was surprised into loud and amazed praise.

"Those are BEAUTIES!" The words tumbled out before Iris could stop them.

Sister smiled at the sincerity and warmth.

And without thinking, she gave them to Iris.

Who was delighted.

"Well," Sister assured her. "There are plenty more. And it has made up for the cabbages failing this year."

Iris had bought cabbage seedlings from

her so she assumed that all her
seedlings had failed to thrive and heart.

As Sister's had.

But no.

"Mine are fine," Iris said. "I lost one,
but the rest have huge hearts."

"Ah well," Sister said.

The islanders found giving hard. Iris
more than most.

And Sister watched then as her guest's
face worked, reddened, laboured. She
saw the struggle to form the words...

"I... I ... I'll GIVE you one,"
exploded.

It had taken nine years of the giving
Sister loved to do to gain this response.

In all those years, this was the first
time this had happened.

Such an effort it was — but she gave,
and a door in her heart opened.

And when the large, hearty cabbage
duly arrived, it was enjoyed to the last
crispy leaf.

Of such "simple" things is the Kingdom
made up.

Of carrots and cabbages given and
received...

Part Three...

...the Fruiting

The Fruiting

Days closing in towards evening now.

Days filled for Sister with gathering
and preserving.

She snatched a day, of rain-washed
quietude amidst fine hectic ones... To
rest, and to read once more.

Sifting through the old papers had
become a pilgrimage in its own right
now.

Rich in memory and prayer.

Outdoors, hedges dripped with
glistening blackberries, and the house
was filled with the drifting, spicy
fragrance of the jam she made from
them.

Rowans for jelly.

Elderberries to mingle in with other fruits.

Apples, crab apples…

Runner beans to dry… or to freeze.

From early to late, Sister's hands were busy garnering and gathering. Her fingers were stained black from the berries, speckled with tiny pricks.

And useless to try to cleanse them until the time was over.

And the greenhouse!

Oh my!

The foliage was so lush and tangled that sometimes, when Sister went in, she expected to find monkeys swinging from the roof supports. To hear gaudy parrots calling.

Beans sprinting and corn rising high... squash and cucumber vines running across the pathways in total unruly abandon...

Was there any end to it all!

All summer there had been food in generous abundance.

Her basket had weighed heavy as every morning she had gathered and garnered, picked and cut.

There was in the harvesting a sweetness that caught at the very soul.

Lord of the Pumpkins,
Lord of the Vines,
Lord of the sweetcorn -
Rich Bread and Wine.

Lord of my Living; Lord of my Giving,
Lord of my weeping; Lord of my
Laughing.

Stay with me, Lord..

And the late months now.

As the season changed, so did the birdsong, and the shapes she saw changed too.

The swallows gathered in the tall trees that sheltered the hermitage, the sound of them almost unbearably poignant.

She watched them practising their flight, bade them eat well...be strong...

And when Hunter Cat one year brought in a dead swallow, still warm, she wept, but marveled at the symmetry and design and colour of the bird.

Skies singing with swallows,
Twittering aerobatics...
Evocative, poignant,
Practising patterns, flight-ready.
Soon, soon to fly, fly, fly,
To warmer shores, where winter-safe.

Winging wide over great oceans,
No footfall pause,
Long, long fasting, striving.

All swooping dots and shapes,
High, high above,
Falling, swooping, lifting then again.
Weaving and whirling in patterns we
know not,

Their lives season knotted,
Tide-tied, moon-tied, seas of mystery...

Short months ago,
Their advent joyed the heart...
Heralds of spring.
Watched for, eagerly vigilled.

In summer, their wild flight-delights
Brought them even in at the door.
The sound of their flight a breath
against the face
As they swept past so close.

Soon now to leave these shores,
Their parting a sign of winter's nearing,
To gather its snug darkness over us.

Part of us with them, the summer-
yearning.

Long, ceaseless flight over wide oceans.

Pilgrims, voyagers, as we,

In trackless wastes of water,
With a sure destination,

Piloted by love.

The pile of papers for autumn was growing. It was an evocative season...

And the quiet work was balm at the ending of a full day.

She would take the cats a walk before dark, gently along the paths, or down to sit by the shore a while.

Nothing strenuous, for she had been on her feet all day.

A tranquil unwinding after fulfilling occupation.

Watching the greenery sear and fade, leaves' falling dance.

Feeling the slight nip in the air that told that frost would not be long in its coming.

Then to light the fire when darkness sweetened the sky.

Waggons of turf had trundled down the steep winding drive, and the peat shed was full to the brim, winter-provided from the very earth.

And thus it was, as the firelight flickered, and the incense of Irish smoke curled up through the chimney, that she came across a reflection written long ago...

Reflection on Saint Francis' Canticle of the Sun.

"Most High, all-powerful, all-good Lord, All praise is Yours, all glory, all honour and all blessings.

To you alone, Most High, do they belong, and no mortal lips are worthy to pronounce Your Name."

At the end of this autumn month. I was garnering leaves in the forest for my new gardens, deep in the silent early day.

Fallen, tumbled gold and russet and orange and brown.

And I stopped in awe.

Just a few months ago, these were buds, then unfolding fresh green to bring us new hope and new strength, spring after winter.

Then full, shading leaves, to give us shelter and coolth in the hot summer days.

And now, their colour dazes and amazes, and, under the top layer as I collect them, are the leaves from past years, turning into rich soil.

Which feeds and nourishes the roots, and helps produce the new leaves that are even now forming in the baring branches.

And this is so year after year; decade after decade, century after century, throughout all the long millennia…

Never failing, faithful, strong, eternal.

"Glory be to the Father and to the Son and to the Holy Spirit, as it was in the beginning, is now and ever shall be, world without end…"

Amen indeed.

And, crouching there as the heavy raindrops fall on the living canopy above me, I am almost in tears at all this. The sheer design and plan in it all.

Nourishment for all our senses, and for our souls. How can we dare and presume to talk to this Creator? To raise our heads to Him? He is all ,and all, and all.

Praise and honour be His…..

We are indeed all unworthy; awed and humbled by His vast love, by His sheer power in lovingkindness..

So we give Him all we are and all we have. Our bodies, our souls, our lives, our love. With wholeheartedness and joy.

And we honour and obey Him and His commandments, without question, on the knees of our souls.

"Praised be You my Lord with all Your creatures, especially Sir Brother Sun, Who is the day through whom You give us light.

And he is beautiful and radiant with great splendour, of You Most High, he bears the likeness."

October flamed in, with strong, robust sun, caressing the land in its fading, comforting, reassuring of love and life.

Its course is lower and briefer now...

125

Strong, sweet, pure as His love...
bright as the days shorten...

And even on dark, wet days, when the
sun and the valley and mountains are
shrouded in grey mist, the sun is there,
as God's love and Presence are there.

Faith is in knowing that as fully when
the sun is hidden as when it shines... as
surely, when we, with our fragile and
fallible senses and weak minds and
erring wills, these "vessels of clay," feel
abandoned by God, as when the
fullness of His love is bright and clear.

"Praised be You, my Lord, through Sister Moon and the stars.

In the heavens you have made them bright, precious and fair."

I have lain in bed, watching a quarter moon, growing, in its course across my window, bright and full and silver, the clouds impossible in their shapes and forms, silvered among the stars.

And, later, a filigree-slender crescent, lying on its back gazing at the stars...

Waxing, waning, drawing tides in that huge mystery of the integrity of creation...

Stars that lead and guide, reminding always of the Christmas star, of the myriad stars God showed to Abraham.

Courses and patterns that have intrigued and mystified men since the beginning of time..

All created by and known to God, safe, sure.

"Praised be You, my Lord, through Brothers Wind and Air,"

Sweet, warm wind, soft and mild, then, later, fierce in the first near-gales of autumn.

The hermitage is tucked snugly into the living breast of the mountain... The air, pure and strong, clean living breath, grass-fragrant...

Always that clear purity of air, sometimes bearing the turf or wood smoke on its breath.

Sometimes rain-laden as autumn moves into winter.

And each direction with its familiar traits. From the south across the wide valley, rattling the front door.

East and it touches not, until I need to go to the mailbox, when I wrap my arms round me against its piercing, west that is gentle, and north that has no fear, for the mountain behind me is a bulwark against it.

And the sea-sound of the wind in the pines echoing in the night.

Strong and free... And still, mist-crowded air, when the valley and mountains, and even the tall alders that fringe this sanctuary, are shrouded and secret.

"And fair and stormy, all weather's moods, by which You cherish all that You have made."

And how varied and multitudinous these moods in these restless months!

And all cherish indeed, for the earth needs the quiet months, needs the heavy rains, needs the winds, to burn off summer, the frost, to kill disease in the soil.

So all is in order, all ordered, all as God has ordained in His love and wisdom.

"Praised be You my Lord through Sister Water, so useful, humble, precious and pure."

And now, the dry weeks of summer are past, and the water flows strong and true.

Serving, cleansing, water of life, streams of living water, as the Bible says so often.

Read Genesis alone and see how the wells are cherished.

Life-nurturers.

Without water in desert lands, death,

Without God, death.

Streams of living waters of Christ...

And the comfort of a hot bath at day's
ending... warming through and through
on chill days... Deep brown off the
high peat bog...

"Praised be You my Lord through Brother Fire, through whom You light the night.

And he is beautiful and playful and robust and strong."

Turf from the high peat bogs, wood from living trees, coal-eggs from a local factory... Burning their generous heat, being consumed as they give of their essence... kettles singing on the hearth, and that living comfort of flame and glow at day's end.

The flicker of flame as I settle to sleep...

An old, old life, as new as each day's fire.

And cats, lined up, as if hypnotised, staring unblinking into the living orange heart of the fire, in the rainy afternoons as I knit and pray.....

"Praised be You my Lord through our Sister, Mother Earth, who sustains and governs us, producing varied fruits with coloured flowers and herbs."

Flowers still; glowing marigolds, nasturtiums, pastel sweet peas, and deeper hues of regal purple.... A few late roses, one by the door, others in the beds...

And bags of apples and pears from the convent's trees.

And the rich variety of jam and juice...
strawberry, gooseberry, blackberry,
crab-apple... And the freezer still full
of fruit and vegetables....

All to be colour and shape to joy the
heart with the knowingness of God's
providing.

And the trees! Again I am inebriated
with the glow of them in this impossibly
beautiful land.

The young ashes here started the month
with acid green and yellow leaves, and
their heavy keys deep brown; now they
are bare, just the bare seeds hanging
down.

"Praise be You my Lord through those who grant pardon for love of You and bear sickness and trial.

Blessed are those who endure in peace, by You Most High, they will be crowned."

And always, here, knowing of those who bear trouble in all its myriad torments.

Praying with and for them... Entrusting them not to human weak and fallible resources, but to Thy strength and light and love, Who alone art holy.

See James… "Patient endurance,"
bearing pain with gladness and with
love, calm and tranquil.

And not bearing grudges, not being
angry, living as we need and seek to be
loved, for love of He Who gave all for
us. Who gave up this sweet and dancing
life on earth at so young an age.

Learning to love from Him.

To forgive as He forgave.

"Praised be You, my Lord through Sister Death, from whom no-one living can escape. Woe to those who die in mortal sin!

Blessed are they She finds doing Your Will. No second death can do them harm."

And always this; this ending of this part of our life.

The first death; death to self when we live in Christ; loving Him and all around us.

Doing His will, living as He did.

So that "second death" is the death of our mortal bodies.

Part of life, part of His work and His creation. To be faced and accepted open-faced.

Strong in the trust of Him, witnessing and with integrity.

"Praise and bless my Lord and give Him thanks, and serve Him with great humility."

For only love humbles; not power, not aggression, not rules and regulations, or discipline.

Simply, purely, wholly, love...

Humility is born of love, not of humiliation, of freedom, not of bondage.

Of being faced with acceptance, not censure.

The open arms of Jesus on the Cross,
not clenched fists or folded arms…

Moses; who sprinkled the Blood of the
Lamb, and we, humbled by seeing God's
living power… humbled before God, yet
lambasting the errant Israelites….

Humility, kneeling before Him in deep
love and awe-ful thankfulness.

AMEN,

AMEN,

AMEN….

It was late now, but Sister's heart was full of memories and thoughts.

And she read now an old story, her heart filling it with more thoughts than were written on the pages...heart thoughts born of compassion and understanding that come with the softening of time.

All the times and people who pass through these lives of ours... shaping by their needs, by their quirks and eccentricities, by the places they live in and the lives they have lived.

Often so hard to live alongside - often harder to be accepted by.

Yet treasured in later times; and would that that treasuring would help us with those we live among later.

"Sing a Song of Harvest Home..."

Sister laughed out loud when she came across the old coloured photos of the island "Harvest Home."

The memories it evoked were rare and fine.

Set as they were in a culture and place all of its own, and utterly different from any other she had ever known.

The only Church on the island was Presbyterian. The Minister, at that time a woman, had to come across by boat on a Sunday to take the service, and again mid week for pastoral and other duties.

Which in winter often did not happen; whereupon one of the islanders led the service, for the half-dozen elderly faithful.

Once there had been a Minister resident, and there were two old ruined Chapels also, as well as the Old Manse, now privately owned, and the New Manse, which was due to be sold.

Along with the doctor's house, the laird's house and one of the laird's tenant farmers, these were almost the only two storey dwellings on the island.

The rest were the long, low stone cottages that hugged the ground, as if for dear life, on an island where gales raged loud and fierce for much of the long, dark winter.

The Church that was used had no electricity, so many of the services in winter were early in the day, or, when the aged ones could not manage the steps, at the school that doubled as a community hall.

The other Churches were far away across the seas, and as there were no boats on Sundays, except sometimes in the summer, to attend Mass would mean two nights away from home.

Sister was of course very self-contained in the hermitage.

And there were occasional visits from the Priest for outlying members of his flock.

And she was...different also.

An incomer, an outlander.

Or as some called such, a "ferry-loper"

And these came and went, and it took time for the decreasing islander families to accept them.

But she gave heartily and joyfully to the various great feasts and festivals observed by all.

The one most beloved of all was the Harvest Home.

It was of course the easiest in so many ways.

Appealing to everyone.

Especially on a small remote island where the ro-ro ferries and electricity were only recently arrived, and where thus more than usual relied on harvests.

Rich and evocative to sight and smell and taste.

The tradition was though fairly new to the island.

Well, the celebration of Christmas was also very new. And for many it did not happen.

It was Hogmanay that mattered.

Christmas was... just another day...

Sister soon altered that for all she knew.

And the hermitage windows glowed with light every December.

When Iris, a non-Church-going neighbour, to rile her, said that Christmas was just a feast of light at the darkest time of year, Sister agreed, and explained to her how Jesus came as the Light of the World.

With such sincerity and joy that Iris never spoke like that before her again.

And became an unusually frequent visitor.

And also with the result that Sister was then invited to join the Women's Guild.

And so it was that she became somehow involved on what was, unbeknown to her, to be her penultimate year on the island, with the preparations for the still-new idea for a Harvest Home.

Being an incomer helped greatly of course, as it was assumed she had great experience of these events.

And Sister soon saw that she might, at last, realize an ambition of hers since childhood.

That one year she had stayed a while, for various reasons, with an old aunt out in the country who had taken her to the Harvest Home at her Church.

More than that, she had taken her to help with the decorating and adorning the day before.

Sister had been entranced as the boxes and bags emptied their bounty and were - more or less - expertly arranged and dispensed with great glee by a whole bevy of ladies, some in their old hats, and many in their flowered pinnies.

A whole sheaf of corn stood tall and proud on the altar steps.

Another was taken apart, and sprays, mingled with Michaelmas daisies, were laid lovingly on each sloping window ledge, and woven through the umbrella holder handles on each of the old carved and polished wooden pews.

Old hands and clumsy knees working away. With a quiet dignity all their own.

That Sister was to remember when her Convent days began.

Old Sisters faithfully working. Honoured and blessing in the seemingly humble tasks, that became mighty through the loving. Teaching by example in loving service.

Apples were polished - and she had chance to help do that as this was her aunt's province.

And she learned that day how rigid the demarcations were there...Let anyone dare tackle another's task...

And the shining apples were carefully added to the windowledges, resting softly shining among the flowers and corn.

Huge displays of dahlias and chrysanthemums on the altar, at the foot of the great brass eagle that was the lectern...

Oh, the rich fragrance of those blooms. Sister could smell it still...

The pulpit, pale stone ornately carved, was a glory of corn and grapes- and a bunch of these was hung from the eagle's mouth also- of fruit and flowers.

Fruit and tinned goods, baskets of brown eggs nestling in golden straw.

Every few minutes the door would open and yet more fruit and flowers would arrive.

To be admired and exclaimed over.

Scrubbed potatoes, carrots glowing orange.

And the marrows! Huge, huge…

And the smell…

Sister's mouth watered as she remembered the fragrance of that Church that morning. Such an aroma of goodness and generosity, of fruit and flowers, with that distinctive autumn tang.

Then she saw the Harvest Loaf...

Oh my!

She stood entranced.

It was propped at the foot of the altar,
and the ladies gathered round it, oohing
and aahing.

Bread, but shaped like a sheaf of corn.
In such detail... Every ear, every stalk,
baked golden brown.

She reached out a longing hand to it,
and her aunt smiled at her wonder.

"Maybe one day you can make one like that!"

For she knew how her small niece loved to bake, and she was teaching her more in these precious weeks together.

The ladies smiled and laughed, not unkindly, and one, "Ah, but Mrs S. always makes the Harvest Loaf." And the lady concerned smiled and nodded her head.

Because it meant a lot to her to do that every year.

And Sister learned that far off day that these customs must be respected and that people had their places and their needs.

And this had stood her in good stead for the Convent, where order reigned, and depended on mutual respect and the quiet Obedience of love.

And the next day, she had sung in wonder as the organ thundered out the old thanksgiving hymns in a Church full to the brim with people.

All dressed in their Sunday best, all singing with zeal and zest.

A mighty hymn of thanksgiving and praise that glowed and soared to heaven.

Her aunt the next day took her once more to the Church.

Again, the faithful, stalwart women were there.

Unsung handmaids, who cleaned and carried all the year round for the Church.

This time though, they were undoing all they had done two days before.

Sister thought how sad it was to take all the decorations apart. It all looked so lovely.

But her aunt carefully and gently explained that there were people in the village and countryside who were not well off, or who were ill, or who were lonely.

So they would make up pretty baskets of fruit and flowers and vegetables to take to them, and Sister could help her aunt to do that.

The next hour was spent so happily, choosing and arranging the produce under her aunt's careful eye. For her aunt knew all the needy ones and what they needed. No use taking a marrow to an old lady on her own, she explained kindly. Better a few eggs and apples.

And the hours after that were spent with her aunt as they drove the lanes to old houses tucked away down half forgotten lanes, to lonely, half-forgotten old ladies.

Sister never forgot how the tired old faces lit up when they saw the basket, and even more when they saw the small child holding it out to them.

That day she learned the need for kindness and caring in lives.

There had of course never been the need or chance to make that Harvest Loaf.

For that was not in their Church tradition.

Nor did she ever attend another Harvest Home like that.

Her aunt had died the following winter, and that autumn remained a golden memory, untarnished by time.

But now, sitting in the turf-hot front room in the small stone cottage where the meetings were held, nibbling home-made cake and sipping coffee, she listened as the ladies planned and claimed their own part in it - just like the ladies in that Church all those years ago...

But so different.

Such a division and awkwardness between the islander women and the incomer women.

It ached Sister's heart.

Finally, she spoke, quietly, and oh so innocently, hoping no one could see the excitement she was feeling.

"I wonder; will we have a Harvest Loaf?"

There was a stunned silence.

Sister realized that maybe they did not even know this tradition.

Her heart soared.

The field was clear...

Yet she would never shame them by letting them know she knew their problem.

"I am happy to make one if no one else wants to?" said diffidently.

They leaped at the offer, most wondering what this southern, outlandish thing could be, but of course not wanting to show ignorance.

And many had cause to know how skilled a baker Sister was...

For her cakes found their quiet way to many a home where there was sickness or sorrow.

So whatever a Harvest Loaf was, it would be fine if it came from her house.

The islanders were good bakers and valued such skills.

So that was settled and agreed.

Sister went home exulting, under the clear skies and starlight.

And the next time she crossed to the mainland to shop, she made sure she had all she needed for this great task.

Enough for a couple or three tries, for suddenly she was nervous.

And, she thought wryly, the hens will appreciate any failures...

And no one will know of course... Hens leave no evidence.

The day before the Church was to be decorated saw Sister up early as ever, working at her self-appointed task even before it grew light.

She mixed and kneaded; that was the easy part that she was used to.

And the rhythm of it soothed and calmed her, and the pleasure came back.

The shaping and "carving" were great fun. Knowing the dough would rise a little before the heat stopped the yeast working.

Sister snipped and plaited, rolled and shaped, using her largest baking tray...

And finally in it went to the hot oven...

And, preceded by the aroma of baking bread, out it came, a glorious sheaf, to be glazed and set to cool.

Sister was delighted.

It looked... like a Harvest Sheaf Loaf.

Sitting there on a large cooling tray on her work top.

It gave Sister such a sense of completion.

Sometimes this does not happen; sometimes when we have thought of doing a special thing for so long, it falls flat.

But Sister's heart was light that day.

She had made a full quantity of dough, so she made a poppy seed plait, and a round cob.

These could go along to give to folk.

She knew that few grew flowers, for the climate was harsh. She had managed to cram an amazing number of plants into her garden, by using containers in every sheltered nook and cranny.

So now with a special thanksgiving in her heart, she went out and cut all she could find.

Bright and gay the box was.

With eggs in an attractive basket.

Sister felt very tired that afternoon, and by nightfall realized she had started a bad cold.

And the following morning, after a restless night, called a neighbour who was in the Guild – which Iris was not of course – and asked her please to take her gifts to the Church as she was not well.

So off the boxes went...and the unwary delight on the faces made Sister smile.

Then she went thankfully to bed - where she stayed on and off for the next week.

Insisting on not infecting anyone, and that she was fine.

So it was only some while later, and from Iris, that she learned the end of the story.

The Church - and she had the photos brought later - looked a picture.

It was a simple building, the plain glass windows showing off the beauty of sky and hill and sea.

And there were flowers everywhere.

And huge cabbages and carrots, which made Sister smile, and eggs.

And there on the table before the pulpit was the Harvest Loaf, flanked by the other two she had sent.

Sister's heart swelled with joy; and oh, she wished her Aunt could see it all.

To give skills is a precious thing indeed.

To give the love we are given by Jesus to others; our carpenter-King.

But when Iris brought the photos, and a small serving of fruit because she had been so ill, she had a light in her eye that Sister was a little wary of.

Knowing Iris's opinion of the Church as she did by now.

And it emerged that there had been awe and admiration for her creative dough... But that the practical islanders, steeped in generations of privation and poverty in that harsh place, had been distressed because they could not decide how it should be eaten.

It had worried them sorely.

Until the minister, a more worldly person who hailed from a great city, hearing of their distress, had rescued them by claiming the Harvest Loaf for the services on the other island she served.

And so Sister's first Harvest Loaf became a much traveled piece of creative doughcraft, amazing islanders on at least two islands, and being a part of the great thanksgiving so humbly and sincerely celebrated.

It reminded Sister, even while when Iris was out of earshot, she laughed until she cried at the pictures the tale evoked, so much of those simple women in her Aunt's Church all those decades ago.

And the words of Jesus echoed in her heart as she fed the hens their evening barley, scattering it like seed.

"Unless ye become as little children..."

These were unsophisticated women in so many ways, as her aunt and her neighbours had been.

Most had hardly left the island where they were born, and the older ones knew life there in a starkness they had survived in.

A generation never to be seen again.

And Sister blessed them in her heart for all they had unwittingly given her in that acceptance of her small offering.

Part Four...

.... the Gift

The Gift

Of course, when Sister searched and retrieved the boxes of Christmas decorations just before Advent, there once more before her eyes were the files of papers.

She had once more had to put them away when the busy-ness of the oncoming winter had made the work once more impossible to complete.

"Three parts done - one to go," she smiled, shaking her head. "Well, as Advent for us is a quiet time, and as all the posting I needed to do is done, maybe this too is a blessing."

For the Nuns spend Advent in silent preparation for the Nativity season. No parties, no Carol Concerts, for Grand

Silence at 7 pm must not be broken.

No huge shopping either, for the Gift of Jesus is enough and more than enough.

A simple feast. A joyous and quiet celebration.

In far lands, where there are desperately poor and homeless, the Sisters work all the while now, to make Christmas special in their giving… Street parties to cook for, toys to collect and gift-wrap, festive hampers to collect for and fill, and make beautiful, for those whose lives hold so little beauty.

So Sister-on-the-mountain has posted parcels that needed to be at the Mother House before Christmas, and her Advent now will be Prayer and thinking

and working ahead for the next year,
her hands busy always.

An antidote to the frenetic pace
elsewhere.

Gentle and quiet and hidden.

These are the gifts the Nuns give to each
other; their loving work a foil to the
Silence and Prayer.

The Silence and Prayer supporting the
giving.

No judging of the ways of others.

Simply a choosing of this their way in
their loving.

So now, the Advent Wreath to make.

Sister set out candles ready. All white.
Four tall, slender ones, and the centre
wide and tall.

A tradition of theirs of great beauty.

And, smiling again, she set the files and
folders on the table.

First, while the light lasted and the rain
held off, out she would go to gather
greenery.

So she wrapped her thick cloak around
her, picked up the wide gathering basket
and secateurs, and, the cats trailing
after her, out she went.

Such luxury and variety there was.

All the traditional, Christmas greenery
there for the picking.

She had already found berried holly on her last shopping expedition, for there was only the green here.

So now she pulled ivy off the ash tree trunks. Sprigs of fir and spruce... Tiny alder cone buds, brown and simple, to set off the green.

Caro leapt of course up the ash tree, closely followed by Amanda. Sturdy, healthy, active cats... rejoicing in air and life. And Sister rejoicing in their joy and zest, laughing as they played and swarmed like small monkeys.

It was mild and sweet, and Sister was reluctant to go back indoors before she needed to.

So she called the cats to her, and set off down the path to the shore.

Soft salt air cool on her face.

They sat a long while there, Sister and her cats.

Just... sitting... Just being.

They curled heavy on her cloaked lap, she resting her veiled head against the tree trunk the bench surrounded.

Watching the light slowly fade over the dove grey skies and the soft, still sea.

Then, as night fell benignly, back up the track to the hermitage.

Checking the sheep had abundant hay and nuts, stroking their bony faces, rubbing behind their ears.

Closing the door on the night and the world then.

Eve of Advent beckoning. With its poignant evocative liturgy.

"In that day the mountains shall drop down new wine, and the hills shall flow with milk and honey, alleluia...
Behold, the Lord our God shall come... and in that day shall be a great light... Ho everyone that thirsteth, come ye to the waters; seek ye the Lord while He may be found, alleluia..."

Then Advent Sunday, and rain falling soft and straight.

Fire fuel heaped high in creels...

First candle lit...

The flame tiny and hesitant at first,
then growing tall and strong and true.

Cats gazing at the fire, their fur too hot
to touch.

The house all tidied for the night.

And Sister found herself restless,
needing some new occupation.

Before beginning the next knitting work.

"Oh, I know! It is so long since I did
any embroidery."

There were just a very, very few she
needed to send cards to, so this year she
would embroider them.

It would not take long, and it would be

a change of occupation…a refreshing thus.

So she fetched the old work basket where oddments of material and threads lay.

Her hands instinctively sought white linen, and red and green thread, and she remembered something she had written years before as she threaded a needle.

And fetched it to re-read.

Being happily waylaid by other pieces…

So many Christmas stories… So much written…

Sister came across an old, yellowed page. Written many years since... Legends and stories from all over the world.

It amazed to see how many everyday creatures and features had been woven into the lore of Christmas.

Nothing left untouched; all is holy...

It matters not if they are objectively "true" for the truth of the eye and heart of faith is its own holiness.

And every tale she read had the same theme. Of giving to the Baby, of feeling how little we have to give, how unworthy the giver feels. Of how their small gift is transformed by the love with which it is offered.

Legend of the Poinsettia

The story is told of Pepita, a poor Mexican child who had no gift to present to the Christ Child at the Christmas Eve service.

As she walked slowly to the Chapel with her cousin, Pedro, her heart was heavy thus.

"I am sure, Pepita, that even the most humble gift, if given in love, will be acceptable in His eyes," said Pedro consolingly.

So Pepita knelt by the path and gathered a handful of weeds, making a small posy of them. It was all she had, but the poverty of her offering shamed her, and she had tears in her eyes as she entered the Chapel.

But as she approached the altar with her gift, she remembered Pedro's words, and her heart lifted as she knelt to lay the flowers at the foot of the Crib.

Suddenly, the bouquet of weeds burst into blooms of brilliant red, and all who saw them were certain that they had witnessed a Christmas miracle right before their eyes.

From that day on, the bright red flowers were known as the Flores de Noche Buena, or Flowers of the Holy Night, today called the poinsettia.

Legend of the Robin..

One story tells of the robin, who was plain brown until the day Jesus was crucified.

The small bird, in compassion, pulled out a thorn from the Crown that was piercing His forehead.

The blood stained the bird's breast for ever, sign of his loving action.

Another tells how, when Jesus was born in bitter cold, the robin fanned the tiny fire with his wings. In doing so, his breast was scorched red.

The Legend of the Christmas Spider

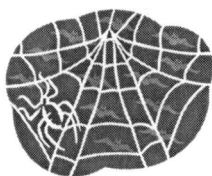

When Joseph and Mary and Jesus were on their way to Egypt, the story runs, as the evening came they were weary, and they sought refuge in a cave. It was very cold, so cold that the ground was white with hoar frost.

A little spider saw the little Baby Jesus, and he wished so much that he could do something for him to keep him warm in the cold night. He decided to do the only thing he could do, to spin his web across the entrance of the cave, to make, as it were, a curtain there.

Along the path there came a detachment of Herod's soldiers, seeking for children to kill to carry out Herod's bloodthirsty order. When they came to the cave, they were about to burst in to search it, to see if anyone was hiding there, but their captain noticed the spider's web. It was covered with the white hoar frost and stretched right across the entrance to the cave.

"Look," he said, "at the spider's web there. It is quite unbroken and there cannot possibly be anyone in the cave, for anyone entering the cave would certainly have torn the web."

So the soldiers passed on, and left the Holy Family in peace because a little spider had spun his web across the entrance to the cave.

And that, so they say, is why to this day we put tinsel on our Christmas trees, for the glittering tinsel streamers stand for the spider's web, white with the hoar frost, stretched across the cave on the way to Egypt.

And here, in Ireland, the old, old custom of leaving a lighted candle in the window on Christmas Eve. To welcome and guide any lost strangers, as Mary and Joseph were guided and welcomed.

With the poignant tradition also that in Penal Times, the candle would indicate a safe place for priests to celebrate the Mass.

Finally Sister tore herself away to read the reflection she had first sought.

The Colours of Christmas

Red, green, white..

The colours of Christmas.

Poinsettias, scarlet against green...
Christmas trees, evergreen... holly, dark,
glossy green with bright red berries...
fireglow... mistletoe, white berries,
whitest snow...

These are the colours of Christmas,
traditional, inherent.

One of the oldest carols; "The holly
bears a berry, as red as any blood"...

And the old carols, singing evocatively
of apple trees, of cherries...of snow...

The colours of Christmas, red, green, white...

Green...growing, renewing, springing, changing.

Green wood, chiselled, sawed into a manger - and a Cross.

Red...life-birthing, life-ending.

But no, you cry?

This is a family time? A warm and glowing time?

For peace and comfort, feasting, love; all things pretty?

Not for death!

And, yes, it is that, all of that - but so much more than that.

Comfort that is real and lasting, rather than illusory and cloying, needs must be founded on and grounded in truth and that fullness of reality that is truth

For if we accept the gold, but not the myrrh, see the pretty baby, but not the pains of that bitter birth, surrounded with rejection and social stigma?

See the Baby-Who-is-God, but not the Man-who-dies-as-God?

We then deny the huge gift given, weaken the grace...trivialise and tame that breathing Spirit, limit and deny God...

Babies; so utterly vulnerable and needy. So defenceless, and defended.

God, in that wooden manger, eliciting and evoking the deepest instincts in us.

And that birth but a beginning, but one stage, begun in the dark warmth of Mary's womb, of a life made to be given fully, in living, but above all in dying.

If it were not for the dying, there would be no rejoicing or thanksgiving in the birthing.

Are we content to accept Him as that Baby, accept Him as a vulnerable youngling?

But not as the One-Who-Died our human death, rejected and scorned?

197

Whose coming in our flesh saved us from all the ills and wrongs done by that flesh?

For every birth is a death too; for death is an integral part of human life - the life that God sanctified by entering into its joys and its pains, all of them from conception to death.

We change; we grow. Baby into child into man...tree into green leaf, then into red berry, and into manger and cross.

Tiny stitches, criss-crossing white fabric with scarlet and green.

The colours of Christmas

The green of promise; the crimson of fulfilment.

In the old carols, the red of cherries and of apples...

The green of tree and holly.

Maybe simply we have lost touch so much with these realities, this rich mingling of life with death, that these things shock and disturb us?

In times past, Masters who painted the Nativity invariably put a crucifix into the scene.

The Baby defeats death; thus the deep joy… God does not deny death; He conquers it.

The cost is blood, His blood.

So; we rejoice, and are at peace.

We revel in the Baby born; knowing that He will die as we die - but not the death that was before He came.

The colours of Christmas...

Green growing.

Red blossoming and fruiting.

The pure, white light of the truth and love of God shining out through that baby, through that star.

And shining out to others through each one of us who accept and embrace Jesus, Baby, Man, Brother, Saviour, Spouse.

Shining clear and strong out into a dark world, spilling light as He spilled His blood.

Candles that are consumed as they shine out for others.

That gift is a challenge. Accepting it will change your life, take you down paths you had not thought to take...

Through the green leafy glades to the scarlet blossoms...

Through life - and through death.

And whatever we give in response to that love, in time, in energy, in skills in money, is so little against what we are given.

Yet because it is given of love, it is all and all and all.

We give not out of obligation or obedience, not constrained or forced, but in sheer exuberant joy and freedom!

That freedom that He gives us in His giving of His life in love for us.

So we give our lives as He gave His, and the love spreads outwards, light radiating into darkness.

Even as the candles burn away they glow warmth and light.

The colours of Christmas...patterned green and red stitches on pure white; tiny crosses, tiny hopes, tiny shoots and fruits.

"The people walking in darkness have seen a great Light: they that dwell in the land of the shadow of death, upon them hath the Light shined...

For unto us a Child is born, unto us a Son is given, and the government shall be upon His shoulder, and His Name shall be called Wonderful, Counsellor, the Mighty God, the everlasting Father, the Prince of Peace."

Verses from Isaiah, Chapter Nine.

Christus Natus Est.....

ALLELUJAH.....

"In the beginning was the Word, and the Word was with God, and the Word was God. The same was in the beginning with God. All things were made by Him; and without Him was nothing made that was made. In Him was Life; and the Life was the Light of men. And the Light shineth in darkness;

and the darkness comprehendeth it not. There was a man sent from God, whose name was John. The same came for a witness, to bear witness of the Light, that all men might believe. He was not that Light, but came to bear witness of that Light. That was the true Light, which lighteth every man that cometh into the world. He was in the world, and the world was made by Him, and the world knew Him not. He came unto His own, and His own received Him not. But as many as received Him, to them gave He power to become the sons of God, even to them that believe in His Name. Which were born, not of blood, nor of the will of the flesh, nor of the will of man, but of God. And the Word was made flesh and dwelt among us, and we beheld His glory, the glory as of the only begotten of the Father, full of grace and truth."

Sister laid aside the pages, and concentrated thoughtfully on the fine stitching in her hands, caught in the pool of bright lamplight, with the fire softly flaming.

And it was Sunday and then another Sunday, and another, before she had chance to return to the papers.

For there was new knitting to work on, a timely lace baby shawl.

That absorbed her time and thoughts...

Somehow, Prayer and Silence for a while meant deeply more than written thoughts.

And she knew that the next story she had found was for nearer the time itself.

So now there were four candles lit...
and it was almost the end of Advent...

She had baked and made all ready,
and was content to sit awhile and
read...

A Christmas Story

for children, and young hearts of all ages.

The Christmas-Tree Angel sneezed, opened her eyes, wished she hadn't - and sneezed again...

All she could see was the moth-eaten, ragged remains of something old and woolly, and very dirty and dusty.

Oh, but not quite all!

That was what had awoken her.

That glimmering shimmer of starlight which somehow had worked through her dismal coverings.

It could only be the Christmas Star - winning through the rags and the grimy skylight...

Christmas!

The Angel struggled to sit up, using her grimy elbows to poke through the smothering rags...

Christmas!

Oh, joy of joys!

Her heart, deep in her cloth breast, swelled and soared...

But where was she?

It must be the attic.

Yes.

But when she had last been put away, the children's loving hands regretful, their mother gently reassuring them that soon, soon, Christmas would come again, all had been neat and clean and orderly.

Now?

Chaos, dirt, disorder...rusty old grates, mouldy old clothes...

And what had happened to her sparkling white dress?

All tattered and filthy…

And her wings!

Oh her poor wings!

All broken...

A tear came to her eye.

And suddenly she heard, oh, sweet sound.

Carols, children's voices, far, far below.

That, too was what had woken her from a long, long sleep.

And the surge of love woke again in her sore heart.

Love is magic; and strong magic indeed on a Holy Night.

For as the Angel had realised, this was indeed that Holiest of all nights.

The Eve of the Nativity.

When God-in-Christ- so- small came
among us...

And she looked down.

And the floors became as glass.

And she could see all the big, tall house
where she had flown at the top of tall,
fragrant Christmas trees, a new,
sparkly dress every year, for many
generations.

All the storeys, and all the rooms, all.

And she realised that she was not in the
old attic.

There all had been clean and neat and
orderly.

212

No; she had been thrust, seemingly with
a lot of rubbish, into a loft above the
attic.

Now, through the floor that had become
as glass, she saw the real attic.

And what she saw made her shiver.

She wrapped a fold of the dirty wool
round her bare shoulders, and gazed
down.

A young man sat there, in collar and tie
and smart trousers, before a large
computer screen full of figures and
formulas.

The room was bare of any tree, or card,
or even a sprig of holly.

Nothing to show that this was the Holy Night.

Bare too of colour and life.

All was glass and chrome, grey and black and white.

The Angel's heart swelled with compassion.

And she peered into his tiny kitchen, so immaculately and unnaturally clean – and so bare and impersonal.

The fridge and cupboards contained not so much as a mince pie or a chicken leg.

Skimmed milk!

Decaffeinated coffee!

Organic cottage cheese!

Broccoli sprigs!

She shook her tattered head, and her halo fell over one eye...

HER children were always full of Christmas!

Of JOY and LIFE.

And their Christmasses celebrated the Coming of Jesus joyously, with feasting and rejoicing.

This poor young man!

A tear fell from her eye - and landed on the young man's head.

Startled, he put his hand up, and wiped the crystal moisture away.

And for a moment his studious, serious face softened - and the carolling grew louder...

Just for a moment the Love broke through.

But the computer bleeped its soulless music and the magic was broken....

And he resumed his gazing and tapping.

The Light was gone from his face.

And the sound of holy singing died away...

And the Angel's eyes were drawn downwards, to the next floor of the rambling old house…

And, oh, such a different scene!

The carols rang loud and sweet and true now!!

There was colour and light; that was her first impression.

A fire burned, and by the hearth, a young mother sat, a baby asleep in her arms, as she watched her children, lovelight in her eyes.

A boy of about six, curly-headed and sturdy, sat, engrossed in colouring cards, at the table.

A younger girl, about three, her hair white-blonde, played with the figures of a Crib, her face animated, her lips moving as she fingered the familiar figures.

A Christmas tree twinkled and glowed joyously in a corner.

And there were bright cards and lovingly- made paper garlands everywhere.

And three stockings hung from the mantlepiece.

The little girl ran to her mother.

"I'm cold, Mummy!"

And as the young mother wrapped her arms of love around her child, the music hesitated, and the Angel saw more clearly.

The fire skulked low and mean in the night chill.

The children were too thinly clad for the winter- time, sleeves too short.

The tree was a tattered old artificial one...

The furniture was shabby and down-at- heel.

With compassion surging, the Angel sought out the kitchen.

Cold, cold, cold.

The tiniest chicken she had ever seen waited in the oven; all legs and bones.

A large pan of potatoes, and carrots enough.

And a small Christmas pudding.

For all these folk?

She saw now how thin the mother was; dark rings under worried eyes.

No father here then.

And no work with a young baby.....

But the love radiating!

The shining of it!

Jenny sent Benjamin, who had also come to her, for the bread.

Making toast on the glowing embers was a warming and absorbing task!

So they gathered in the fireglow...

The Light in their hearts and on their faces.

And Jenny fed her babe, an ache in her heart.

Jeff had died too suddenly and too unexpectedly to have made provision for his young family.

And he had been struggling to set up in business, a calculatedly lean time for them.

So it was a struggle now, with the new baby too..

Sighing, the Angel looked down, as the threadbare rug on the cold lino became as glass.

And she blinked at what she saw!

Opulence, luxury!

A big log-effect electric fire blazed in
the hearth, and radiators pulsed heat.

Rich, thick carpets, deep soft armchairs,
and the sheen of highly polished wood.

A huge tree, redolent of pine, and
shining and shimmering with long-piled
tinsel and glass ornaments.

Fruit in crystal bowls; expensive
chocolates...

And by the fire...

One small person?

An old lady, a glass in her hand,
expensively dressed and coiffeured....

But where was the happiness?

The carols were silent now, for there
was not here that love they needed to
sing in...

Her face held no happiness.

No Light here.

The Angel looked in the kitchen.

Oh, so warm and fitted with all manner
of devices.

And the large fridge groaning and
packed.

Cheeses of every nation,

Cream.

Pate and sausage...

Ham....

And a small but plump turkey nestling, well-stuffed, among tiny sausages and bacon rolls...

And desserts!

Ice-cream...

Cream filled eclairs jostled and elbowed each other in the freezer...

A large, elaborately iced cake...

Tins of shortbread and chocolate biscuits....

The Angel fairly bristled with indignation!

There were those little cherub-mites, a few feet above all this rich indulgence, making toast with the cheapest bread, on a tiny fire!

Cuddling together for warmth...

And that young man!

Ignorant and insouciant, lost in his tiny, unreal electronic world...

She frowned, an idea birthing in her...

And as she pondered, the compassion radiated and spread out from her in that love that is itself the strongest prayer there is.

Selfless and reaching out...

Her heart almost burst with that love.

And outside, unforecast, unheralded by
mortal meteorologists, snow began
falling.

Christmas snow, thick, soft, veiling the
human harshness of the world,

Cloaking all with the silence and purity
of Heaven.

Large shining flakes, dancing in
Heaven's ageless rhythms...

And the carols soared and gathered
power.

Why, the very angels sang with them.

Voices sweet and pure and holy...

The saints in heaven gathered, singing,
carolling, and watched, breath bated,
prayer a tangible incense now...

All focussed on this tall house and its
people...

For God is a God who loves each soul
as the good Father He is...

And the Angel, love strong in her cloth
breast, hurt for the hurt, cold for the
cold, grieving for the grieving,
shuddered with adoration and longing..

And the snow fell heavy, heavy,
heavy...

And the power lines sagged, sagged,
sagged.

The young mother, her three children gathered around her, folded under her blue shawl like chicks under a hen's wings, gazed into the embers of the fire...

The young man stretched and yawned, thinking of his bed...

The old lady sipped her drink and closed her eyes...

And with a silent exultation, as silent as the Birth that night, the world man had made went suddenly dark...

As the power lines refused to accept the weight of the thick, thick snow.

No street lights...

Only the Christmas starlight, the huge, lambent winter moon.

And that one, huge, radiant star...

Outshining all the rest...

The mother and her children did not even notice that the power had gone.

They were engrossed in toast and love!

Warm together by the firelight and candle-light, safe in their loving ...

The young man was terrified!

His whole world, in his close-curtained attic, suddenly went black..

Then he realised, through his panic, that it was a power cut.

He had never thought to buy candles or a torch.

So he groped his slow, clumsy way across to the window.

Loud agony as he stubbed his toes on the inimical, angular edges of his cold, metal furniture.

And the sight when he pulled the thick curtains aside took his unwary breath away.

A white, bright world...

No lights made by man.

Starlight.

Silence.

And that huge, huge smiling moon over the pure, still world.

He stood, mesmerised...

The old lady was startled beyond measure.

Suddenly her luxurious nest was dark.

And it began to grow very cold amazingly quickly...

She shivered in her fashionably thin clothes...

She thought longingly of bed - but the electric blanket would not be on, and fine linen sheets are very cold...

All her home was electric.

Not so much as a gas ring...

Not a candle to be had...

Memories of a long-ago childhood began to steal into her mind.

A poor home - and a poverty she had vowed never to be near again.

But there had been warmth of a different kind, she realised, with a sudden pang...

Too many children, too few clothes, too little food, and that poor.

But, oh the love!

Tears pricked at her lonely eyes —

And suddenly she heard a baby cry...

And, for the first time, she thought of the young family upstairs.

She, being on the ground floor, and with her own entrance, had found it easy to avoid contact.

She had no idea how they lived, frowned at childish noise...

But how would they cope?

The young man heard that thin wail too.

He also had avoided contact with the other residents.

Sometimes, inevitably, they met on the stairs, but he rushed past, always in a hurry to get to his computer..

But also, and he knew this now with a painful clarity, because in the Children's Home he had been brought up in, there had been too many kids, far too many, and too little affection.

Always someone else needing and getting attention, until he gave up seeking any.

He lost himself first in books, then in his electronic world, at work and at home...

Suddenly, the light of that bright Star entered his soul...

At the same time as it did the old lady's...

Oh the power of helplessness!

The strength of the thin cry of a tiny baby!

The old lady and the young man met at the door of the flat where the young family were wrapped and enfolded in warmth..

The moon beamed in on them, its silvery light ghostly and unreal.

They looked sheepishly at each other - and started talking at the same time...

"I just wondered…"

"The baby…"

And the young mother heard them, and opened the door hesitantly.

The baby was held in her blue-shawled arms.

The candlelight flickered around her with the sudden movement of air.

The two neighbours gasped.

For Love at Christmas is tangible…

Especially where a mother and baby are…

Here were they, cold and dark on the

landing, their rich homes dark and empty.

And here were these, in a warm, light sanctuary...

Jenny, of course, solicitous, invited them in as soon as she heard about the power cut.

Love is mother to all.

She shooed them gently to the fire.

And set the kettle to boil on the old gas cooker for a pot of hot tea...

And set Benjamin to making more toast.

She opened the precious pot of honey she had been saving...

And put more scarce coal on the fire...

Lit more candles...

For every stranger in need is the Christ-Child.

Becky, her mother's daughter, once her short shyness had worn off, snuggled up to Miss Marsh.

That contact with the physical warmth of the loving, unjudging child took the old lady's breath away...

And Benjamin showed his craft work to Colin...

And engrossed him in the intricacies; a sharing that was full and whole.

And the young man's lonely heart began to mend.

And the carols soared outside.

And no-one thought to wonder who was out there in the thick, thick snow.

For Christmas magic was too strong now for human minds to question.

And they all, replete and warm, joined in...

Becky by now was snuggled on Miss Marsh's unaccustomed lap.

Benjamin and Colin, the boy and young man side by side on the settee...

Miss Marsh and Colin were spellbound...

But could not help but notice how worn and thin all was.

How little this loving and generous family had...

And Miss Marsh found herself thinking about her home.

Of all she had ready there.

Of the rich, abundant food...

She cleared her throat nervously - for she realised that this poor family was

rich in ways she could never aspire to,
and needed not her bounty...

"I was wondering... how would you
like to come to me tomorrow? For

Christmas dinner, I mean? All of
you?"

And she smiled at Colin also.

There was silence...

The very carols paused in mid-verse..

Becky broke the awkwardness she in
her child-likeness had no awareness of.

In her simplicity there were no
overtones, no subtlety of undercurrents...

"PLEASE, Mummy! I love Miss Marsh!"

Jenny's gaze was keen. If this was charity...

But the carols started again, and she saw with sudden clarity the lonely lines on the old face... and the lostness in the young man's eyes...

And she smiled.

A Christmas smile...

She had so little to give - but she had all.

So much love in these small, giant souls!

"Oh, that would be lovely! But you have no electricity! And it will be so cold down there. And who knows when the power will be back on?"

Miss Marsh knew a keen, sharp pang of pain and disappointment.

Then Colin, to whom the idea of Christmas had set off a train of longing, cleared his throat and spoke.

"Well, this is just an idea - and I have no Christmas stuff in, but if Jenny will agree, can we not - pool resources?"

Miss Marsh's face cleared, relief dancing through her.

"Yes of course! If Jenny will agree, I can bring all the food here. And we can cook it together?"

So that is what they did.

Miss Marsh and Colin went home clutching hot water bottles.

And in the snow-cold of that Christmas Day, they met to go to Church - for Jenny insisted they share all...

And each heart was thankful.

The snow had stopped, and the sun dazzled and radiated prisms and rainbows off the piled banks and ripples of it.

All the men had turned out with spades and shovels to clear paths on the pavements.

Colin had worked with them and his face shone with the air and exertion

There was still no power, but the Church was bright.

The sun glowed and rainbowed through the stained glass.

And darker corners were alive with candles.

For all who came brought them.

Small lights to make a great Light.

And all shared and smiled with a joyous camaraderie...

And the children, flanked by the adults, gathered round the Crib.

They celebrated the Coming of Jesus with whole hearts and strong voices.

And then a procession! The turkey was already sizzling in Jenny's oven.

And now they carried all the good things down, until the old table fairly groaned.

The children's faces were a picture!

Colin vanished, to return with a whole sack of coal, and bags of logs; an enterprising shop had opened its doors. ..

Boxes of candles.

And a bright jigsaw...

And the flat rang with laughter.

Delicious, rich aromas rose to heaven...

The Christmas-Tree Angel yawned and drooped.

Her mission accomplished, she was exhausted.

And as the winter afternoon early darkened into evening, she knew that her time was ending...

Indeed, she had had an extension, for

249

Christmas-Tree Angels only come to life on Christmas Eve...

She gazed with love on the people below her, drinking in the glad faces, replete with more than good food...

Colin, working with Benjamin on the jigsaw...

Jenny nursing baby Jeff, his small face upturned to her.

Miss Marsh sharing the Crib with Becky...

The candles casting their soft light.

The logs blazing their living warmth.

Oh, it was so good; all so good!

And it was a love that would last, and grow and heal its givers and receivers...

Then, she started to feel...different

Instead of fading, she was coming to life in a new way...

She blinked...

And as she watched, her tattered, torn, dirty old dress began to change..

White, long, radiant…

Clean, pure...

And her shoulders began to prickle...

And her head felt different...

And the dirty skylight cleared, seemed to open...

Wide onto the starry heavens...

And the light from that bright star grew and radiated outwards.

Wider and wider

And brighter and brighter.

Until it encompassed and embraced all, all, all...

And oh!

The Christmas-Tree Angel...wide new, feathered wings outspread.

White gown flowing.

Bright-haloed head.

She floated and flew out, up.

The newest angel in God's Heaven...

To be where there is no rust or moth.

No cold or darkness...

No pain or sorrow.

Just pure Light.

Shining out from the Christ Child.

To all and through all who love Him.

Radiating out into the whole world.

Light and love and peace...

Jesus. Light of the World. ....Way,
Truth, Life...

* * * * *

Sister gazed into the glowing heart of
the turf fire.

It was Christmas Eve, dark now, and
the last of the Carols from King's had
echoed and faded away.

And this year even they had seemed
somehow intrusive.

The day had held surprises. Two from
the village had called, bearing gifts of
seasonal food for her.

As if someone had told them that there
had been a feeding crisis overseas, and,
like all her Sisters, she had sent all the

money she could, including the small sum intended for some small Christmas treats.

There was always food in the house.

And it was no great worry.

But always there was loving provision, and now, through the kindness of others, rushing round on Christmas Eve, there was all anyone could wish for, even a small turkey.

She had pondered on going down to Mass.

But then, before the Carols began, the heavy sky had sent the first snowflakes. And by darkfall, there was the crystal beauty of a few inches of pure white.

So, in tranquillity, she was effectively cut off from the village now. Set apart from the world outside the hermitage.

And now she simply sat, even her hands still, by candle and firelight, utterly content to be where she was and who she was.

Keeping Vigil, a small light up on the mountain.

Postscript...

And so the year passes, and the years pass.

For Sister-on-the- mountain, and all her Sisters, wherever and however they live this life, the sweetness of hands busy, giving skills lent to them, and passing then that bright torch of loving and surrendering on.

Seasons and years...

Old Nun, in springtime sun..
Her music the birds' sweet orison...
Fingers flying through fine cream wool...
A shawl for a baby she will never see,

Far away across the sea...

Old Nun in summer rain,
Watching the streaming window pane,
Hands working a rainbow of mitts,
For winter- children she will never see,
Far away across the sea...

Old Nun in autumn gales,
Seeing the green world fade and pale,
Lap heaped high with thick warm hats,
For old and cold she will never meet,
Far away across the sea...

Old Nun in winter snow –
Homeward-bound.. not far to go.
Winding white wool ....slow, pensive
hands,
Rapt in the dove-wings heavenly
dance...
To be worked by Sisters she will never
see...

Far away across the sea...

Seasons of soul, seasons of heart,
Seasons together, seasons apart...

Rain and snow, wind and rain...
Mattering nothing, the ache or the
pain....

Always the Son, always that gain
Of love given freely, of life fully
shared,
Of heaven on earth, of Jesus in heart.

Always the love, that bright, strong-
wrought thread...

Enfolding, embracing, a healing of
heaven.

Many times are we asked, how we began, who was our Foundress, the where, the when... the why.

Many times there has been the intention to write all these things and more, but always there are other things.

For hungry children come before all else.

And when the Order almost died out a score or more years ago, all the records were left in a damp cellar in England.

They were, in that sad state, taken to Canada when the Mother House moved there, and when our Convent there was washed away by floods, once more they were saturated.

The task of trying to salvage the papers is a time consuming and heart breaking one.

For we cannot afford to get this done professionally.

But we have also many memories passed down orally...

And so now "The Legend of Mother Luke" is being written, and will be published later.

We offer here a summary of that inspiring and fascinating work.

The Legend of Mother Luke...

.... being the story of Sisters of Grace.

Once upon a time, there was a young girl who loved Jesus more than she loved her life, and longed to serve Him in the poor with all her heart and soul and mind and strength.

When she was only sixteen, she ran away from her rich home, for she was gently and nobly born, to earn her own living, so she could give all she earned to the very poor who thronged the streets.

For she knew that if she stayed where she was, soon she would be married off...

And the Spouse she sought was Jesus Christ.

Had she entered a convent, her contact with the poor would be strictly limited, and that was not what Jesus was asking of her.

She worked in a noisy, dirty factory by day and served the street people after the long hours there.

Soon they knew her goodness and kindness, that she was one of them and kept nothing back for herself.

And she took Vows with a Priest and then was later Consecrated as Abbess.

For very soon more women sought her out to live with her, and to do the work for Jesus she was doing.

And so the Order was founded.

To own nothing, not a house to live in, not a big convent separating them from the people they served.

Like Jesus, as He teaches in Matthew, they carried nothing for their journey.

Beyond what they needed, they had nothing.

They put on the Holy Habit of Religion. Now everyone saw who they were and knew who they could turn to for sustenance and the lovingkindness of the Lord Jesus.

They lived at first on the streets with those they were supporting. Like Jesus, they had nowhere to lay their heads.

They were not like Nuns from a Convent, who visited the poor then went back to their House.

To earn money to feed the homeless ones they would gather fruit, anything that would sell, and sit on the street with a barrow.

Earning all they gave and giving all they earned.

Then one day a lady came to them. She knew the work they did and how poorly they lived.

She had been left a small cottage, and God told her in a dream to give them this inheritance.

That little, simple House became a

House of Grace; the grace of Jesus providing for his Brides.

There the first Sisters lived, twelve in harmony, and from there Sisters over long years went out, two by two, taking nothing, for they had nothing, to parishes throughout the land, and some overseas.

There too Sisters were formed and trained.

From all classes and walks of life.

All this was almost 150 years ago, in the south of England.

And as years and decades passed, the way they lived stayed strong and true.

Always reliant on the work of their hands, and on benefactors. On God providing daily for their needs.

For they were not allowed to own property, or to keep money in the bank, even if they had any.

All went to the very poor and hungry.

As it still does.

They never had any "old money" thus; never any coffers to fall back on.

Wherever they lived, they grew food and worked at whatever they could to earn their keep and feed the hungry.

Determined, loving Jesus, and living His teachings.

Prayer always their support and strength.

And always, God met their needs.

So they would see an empty house, that was not needed or used, and ask for it.

Not to own it; but simply to use and care for it.

Sometimes a house they rented would be lent to them; to be used by the Order as long as it existed.

Or used for a set time, say five years, after which they would own it and could sell it if they needed to.

Is that a huge thing to ask?

To use a piece of land that is sitting idle? To live quietly in prayer in a house that no-one needs?

Now these Sisters are in great and urgent need here once more. Of a quiet place where they can live and use their skills to feed the victims of terrible disasters. Names like tsunami, Myanmar, echo in the heart and will do for many years.

They yearn to do more, but they need here a base, a safe sanctuary. A refuge where they can live in peace and grow food and emerge from for their work.

They ask nothing more than that, and they would then become invisible – until and unless there is need of their skill and their work.

And then they will respond generously and without stint.

For their original charism stands faithful and true.

It has not changed.

Still dependent on divine providence working through the people of God to reach out in help to the people of God.

Still each and all working every hour they can to feed and clothe Jesus.

Email us on
anchoresscj@yahoo.com

Blessings heap upon you...

Tales from an Irish Hermitage

by a Nun of Grace

A charming collection of tales from Ireland, where a Nun makes room for the sheep, hens, geese, and others nobody else wants.

Order from
www.xanga.com/sistersofgraceofchrist

Or email Sisters of Grace at
anchoresscj@yahoo.com

Printed in the United Kingdom
by Lightning Source UK Ltd.
130864UK00001BB/1-54/P

9 780980 931716